THE CREATIVE COOK

Easy & Artful

Asian Cooking

RICHARD CAWLEY

Foreword By KEN HOM

COLE
GROUP

Please note the following:

Quantities given in all the recipes serve 4 people unless otherwise stated.

Butter and margarine are packaged in a variety of forms, including 1-pound blocks and ¼-pound sticks. A stick equals 8 tablespoons (½ cup).

Cream used is specified as light cream (containing from 18 percent to 30 percent milk fat), whipping cream (30 percent to 36 percent milk fat), or heavy cream (at least 36 percent milk fat).

Flour used is all-purpose flour, unless otherwise specified.

Preparation of ingredients, such as the cleaning, trimming, and peeling of vegetables and fruit, is presumed and the text refers to any aspect of this only if unusual, such as onions used unpeeled, etc.

Citrus fruit should be thoroughly washed to remove any agricultural residues. For this reason, whenever a recipe uses the rind of any citrus such as oranges, lemon, or limes, the text specifies washed fruit. Wash the fruit thoroughly, rinse well, and pat dry. If using organically grown fruit, rinse briefly and pat dry.

Eggs used are large unless otherwise specified. Because of the risk of contamination with salmonella bacteria, current recommendations from health professionals are that children, pregnant women, people on immuno-suppressant drugs, and the elderly should not eat raw or lightly cooked eggs. This book includes recipes with raw and lightly cooked eggs. These recipes are marked by an ★ in the text.

Editorial Direction: Lewis Esson Publishing
Art Director: Mary Evans
Design: Sue Storey
Illustrations: Alison Barratt
Food for Photography: Richard Cawley
Styling: Róisín Nield
Editorial Assistant: Penny David
American Editor: Norma MacMillan
Production Manager: Sonya Sibbons

Text copyright © Richard Cawley 1993
Foreword copyright © Ken Hom 1993
Photography copyright © Michelle Garrett 1993
Design and layout copyright © Conran Octopus 1993

Published by Cole Group
4415 Sonoma Highway/PO Box 4089
Santa Rosa, CA 95402–4089
(707) 538–0492 FAX (707) 538–0497

First published in 1992 by
Conran Octopus Limited,
37 Shelton Street, London WC2H 9HN

A	B	C	D	E	F	G	H
3	4	5	6	7	8	9	0

ISBN 1–56426–654–0
Library of Congress Cataloguing in process

Typeset by Servis Filmsetting Ltd
Printed and bound in Hong Kong

Distributed to the book trade by Publishers Group West

CONTENTS

FOREWORD

This collection of recipes is a welcome addition to that genre of modern cooking that emphasizes simplicity and ease of preparation, without, however, any sacrifice of quality or delectability. There is no implication of the blandness and uniformity of "fast food" here. All of Richard's recipes are well thought out, preserving the tastes and textures of the original cuisines. He has omitted or refashioned the more elaborate and time-consuming recipes in order to expedite the preparation of dishes and menus that capture the representative qualities of each cooking style. The essence remains intact; only the time element has changed.

Cooking quickly and easily, without compromising quality, comes naturally to those who spend a good deal of time in the kitchen. Of course, elaborate, multi-course dinners take much time and effort. But not every meal is a major social or family event, no cook *always* has enough time, and, sometimes (perhaps more often than not) a quick, easy meal is just the right thing – as long as it is also delicious. This book captures that spirit.

It is obvious that *Easy & Artful Asian Cooking* is the fruit of many years of rich experience and successful experimentation in the kitchen. The recipes manifest Richard's personal style and good taste. I love his approach to the venerable traditions of Asian cooking. That is to say, he understands and respects both the process and the final results. As Richard's long career of writing about food

exemplifies, there is nothing mystical about preparing the good foods of many cuisines. The art of masterful cooking requires practical understanding of both techniques and ingredients. Richard's ability to convey this understanding is one of his strong virtues.

As I peruse the recipes, many of which are familiar to me – albeit in Richard's own form – I see that he has succeeded in simplifying both the preparation and the ingredients without losing anything essential. His emphasis on freshness of ingredients and his selection of dishes that require only a few basic sauces and the most readily available seasonings together ensure that the results will be delicious and true to the original.

Let me commend, too, Richard's reliance in all of these recipes on traditional Asian spices, seasonings, and sauces. These are essential if you are to experience authentic Asian cuisine. All the ingredients used in this book are, fortunately, easily available today. So take your time shopping for these exotic items, and savor the adventure. Once you have stocked your pantry with the basics, you are halfway there. You need only accumulate experience and develop confidence. Using Richard's recipes as your point of departure, you will be on your way to the enjoyment of authentic healthy, tasty Asian food. I wish you good health and delicious meals!

KEN HOM

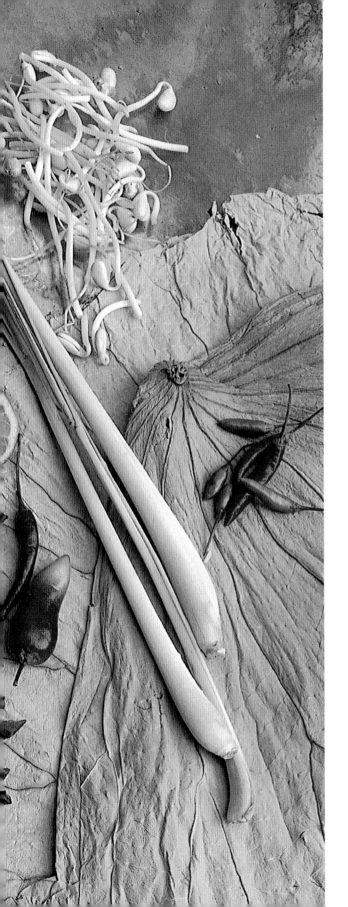

INTRODUCTION

Some years ago, I spent three months traveling in China, from the great cities of Shanghai and Beijing, down the Yangtse River to the end of the Great Wall on the edge of the Gobi Desert.

There were four of us, and twice a day we would order a meal consisting of five or six different dishes – over eight hundred dishes in all – and yet hardly ever did we eat the same dish twice. Chinese cooking is probably the oldest real cuisine in the world and perhaps this is the reason for its extraordinary variety.

The Chinese have always been great merchants and colonizers, and their influence has spread all over Southeast Asia – in the culture and food of Thailand, Malaysia and Singapore, in Korea and Japan, and southeast to the 14,000 or so islands of the Indonesian archipelago.

Within China, the ingredients and flavors of food vary enormously, from mild and fragrant to pungent and fiery. In the south, rice is the staple food, while in the colder wheat-growing northern regions, rice is largely replaced by bread and noodles. In kitchens throughout this vast country, three basic ingredients are as essential to a Chinese cook as salt and pepper are to us – garlic, ginger, and soy sauce.

Chinese – and indeed most Asian food – generally takes much longer to prepare than it does to cook. In densely populated areas, the most effective way to get the best value out of small quantities of expensive fuel is to cut ingredients into small, uniform, bite-sized pieces, so that they need only very brief cooking. The curved-bottomed wok was developed to use the minimum amount of fat or oil and cook in the fastest possible time over the first fierce heat from a small quantity of blazing charcoal. As the coals cooled to a gentler glow, they would be economically used to cook steamed and braised dishes. Deep-frying and barbecuing complete the repertoire of classic Asian cooking methods. Roasting and baking, which require an oven and large quantities of fuel, are hardly used at all.

The other main characteristic that distinguishes Chinese cooking is that of achieving harmony through contrast. This applies not just to the taste of food, but to its texture, shape and color. Chinese food must please the eye as well as the palate. Japan and Thailand refined the presentation of food even further, almost to the point of being an art form.

Even though Chinese preparation techniques and cooking methods have been absorbed by the cuisines of so many other countries, each one has added its own character and personality, influenced by climate, population, and local ingredients.

Religion has also played a part in shaping some Asian cuisines. For example, most Indonesians are Muslim and shun pork, which is so greatly loved by the Chinese. Luckily, Indonesians can take advan-

tage of the wide variety of fish from the surrounding seas. This is sometimes cooked very simply, but is often flavored with various spices – the Indonesian archipelago was, after all, once known as the Spice Islands.

In China, most food is cooked, though often very briefly. Hardly anything is eaten uncooked. However, the Japanese are passionate about raw food, especially fish and – unlike the Chinese – they also eat salads, as do the Thais, who make theirs from delicious combinations of meat and fish with fruit, vegetables, and herbs. Fragrant herbs and spices, fiery chilies, pungent fish sauces, and creamy coconut all help make Thai dishes distinctive.

Each Asian cuisine holds its own variety of particular delights, with the added attraction for modern Western cooks that an Asian-style diet is light and healthy, being based on rice or noodles with little fat and sugar and lots of nutritious fresh vegetables and fruit. The small quantities of meat, fish, and poultry that are featured on Asian menus also mean that it is a relatively inexpensive way to eat.

ABOUT THE RECIPES

This book presents recipes from all over the Southeast Asian area, with the idea of trying to offer as much variety as possible. Many of the recipes are classics, while others are adapted slightly to make them as easy as possible to cook, or to avoid difficulty in obtaining unusual ingredients. A few are my own East-meets-West favorites.

Unlike the Western habit of eating a meal of separate courses where one course follows another, most Asian meals consist of a large communal serving of rice or noodles with a series of "made" dishes brought to the table all at the same time. If soup is included, it may also be served at the same time to be enjoyed throughout the meal, rather than as a first course.

The idea of this book is that you should mix and match whichever dishes you want, in whichever order you like – or all at once in the style of a Chinese banquet. Don't feel you should choose all the dishes from one area – it is interesting and fun to mix dishes from different countries in one meal.

Do try and select recipes that will give you "harmony through contrast," but be careful not to choose too many dishes that require last-minute cooking. Many dishes – especially soups, salads, and dishes cooked in sauces – can be prepared a little in advance to help spread the workload. A menu consisting solely of deep-fried and stir-fried dishes will not leave the cook much time to sit down and enjoy the food or company.

If you are new to this kind of cooking, perhaps you might like to try just one or two Asian dishes to begin with, incorporating one dish at a time into a Western-style meal. Try serving a Chinese soup or a Thai salad as an appetizer before a traditional roast dinner, for instance. If you fancy mashed potatoes with spareribs instead of rice, go ahead – remember food is to be enjoyed.

If you are undecided what to drink with an Asian meal, the safest bet is cold beer, as it will not be overpowered by spicy flavors in the way that a delicate wine might be. Dry sherry – which is very like Chinese wine, is excellent served with snacks and appetizers at the beginning of a meal. Chinese tea and mineral waters make good non-alcoholic alternatives.

INGREDIENTS AND EQUIPMENT

Most of the ingredients used in these recipes can be found in large supermarkets, and most large cities now have an Asian market. If you have trouble finding any of the more unusual items, a variety of mail order catalogues can supply anything you might need. You will find notes on some of the more unusual ingredients alongside the appropriate recipes, plus some suggested substitutes.

Many of the recipes include fresh chili peppers. There are many different sizes, shapes, and colors of chilies available and all vary in "heat." As a general rule, the smaller they are, the more fiery their flavor. The only certain way to find out is to taste a tiny piece and judge for yourself how much to put in. The quantities given in the recipes are only suggestions, and whether you choose to use more or less is a matter of taste. The seeds are the hottest part of the chili, so it is advisable to remove these during preparation. It is also a good idea to wear rubber gloves when preparing chilies, as the slightest touch of a "chili finger" on eyes, or other sensitive parts of the body, can cause extreme discomfort. Otherwise, be sure to wash your hands carefully after handling the chilies.

A wok is almost essential for cooking most Asian dishes. Comparatively cheap woks are, however, readily available in most cookware stores and prove invaluable in the kitchen for all kinds of cooking apart from just Asian recipes. Stir-frying with a wok is a very healthy way to cook as it uses very little oil. The important thing to remember when using a wok is to heat it well before putting in the oil. Wait until you can feel the heat radiating from the bottom of the interior when you place your hand about 3 inches above it. When deep-frying in a wok, pour in enough oil to give a depth of about 2 inches and heat it over medium heat until you can just see a faint haze of smoke rising from it, before putting in the food to be fried. Cook the food in fairly small batches so that the wok is not over-crowded and the food doesn't cool the oil too much when it is added.

So stock your pantry with a few Asian herbs, spices, and condiments; pile your shopping cart with delicious fresh ingredients; get out your wok; and fill your kitchen with the delicious aromas and flavors of the Orient.

Thick, sweet-spicy Plum Sauce *is traditionally served by the Chinese as a dip with dumplings or seafood and with poultry dishes, especially duck.* Asian Pickled Plums, *preserved in a spiced vinegar, are available from Asian markets. A blender or food processor easily gets the peppers minced to the correct degree of fineness.*

Sambals *are Indonesian relishes, usually spiced with chili peppers.*

PLUM SAUCE

MAKES ABOUT 5 CUPS

2 oz Asian pickled plums
2¼ cups sugar
2–3 large hot red chili peppers, seeded and minced
1 red sweet pepper, seeded and minced
¼ cup rice or white wine vinegar

Rub the plums through the fingers to break up the flesh, but do not discard the pits.

Put the sugar and 1¼ cups of water in a saucepan and bring to a boil over medium heat. When the syrup is boiling well, add the chili peppers, the sweet pepper, and the plums with their pits. Bring back to a boil and boil 2–3 minutes, then stir in the vinegar. The resulting sauce will be sweet-and-sour.

Let cool, then remove and discard the pits. Pour into warmed sterilized bottles or jars and seal or stopper tightly. This sauce will stay fresh for several weeks in the refrigerator.

CUCUMBER AND CARROT RELISH

MAKES ABOUT 1½ CUPS

2 tbsp sugar
juice of ½ lime
¼ English cucumber, minced
2 shallots, thinly sliced
1 small carrot, grated
1 large hot red or green chili pepper or more to taste, seeded and minced

In a small bowl, dissolve the sugar in 2 tablespoons of hot water. Mix in all the other ingredients.

Chill for at least 1 hour to let the flavors develop fully, but use within 24 hours.

PEANUT AND PEPPER RELISH

MAKES ABOUT 1 CUP

¾ cup chopped salted peanuts
½ red or yellow sweet pepper, seeded and minced
½ tsp curry powder
1 small garlic clove, minced
3 tbsp thick plain yogurt
2 tbsp chopped fresh flat-leaf parsley

Mix all the ingredients and chill at least 1 hour, or up to 24, to let flavors develop fully.

MANGO SAMBAL

MAKES ABOUT 1½ CUPS

½ large ripe mango, peeled and coarsely chopped
2 scallions, thinly sliced
⅛ English cucumber, coarsely chopped
1 hot chili pepper, seeded and minced
juice of 1 lime or lemon
1 heaping tbsp chopped fresh cilantro

Combine all the ingredients except the cilantro and chill at least 1 hour, or up to 24, to let the flavors develop fully.

Just before serving, mix in the cilantro.

COCONUT SAMBAL

MAKES ABOUT 1½ CUPS

1 cup freshly grated coconut (not packed)
½ small mild onion, thinly sliced
1 hot chili pepper, seeded and minced
juice of 1 lime or lemon
¼ tsp salt

Mix all the ingredients well and chill at least 1 hour, or up to 24, to let the flavors develop fully.

SPICED BANANA SALAD

SERVES 4 AS AN ACCOMPANIMENT

2 tbsp unsalted butter
1 tsp black cumin seed
¼ tsp chili powder
2 firm bananas, peeled and cut into ½-inch slices
2 small heads of Belgian endive, separated into leaves
1 small mild onion, very thinly sliced and separated into rings
¼ cup plain yogurt
salt
cayenne pepper

Melt the butter in a frying pan over medium heat and sauté the cumin and chili powder 2 minutes.

Add the banana slices and fry 2–3 minutes, turning once. The banana should be soft and hot, but still hold its shape.

Arrange the endive leaves on 4 small plates or bowls, radiating out from the center. Add the onion rings and the warm banana and sprinkle with salt to taste.

Top with the yogurt, sprinkle with cayenne, and serve immediately.

NOTE: Alternatively, present the entire dish on one large serving platter. Serve as a side dish with any curry.

Clockwise from the top: Coconut Sambal, Mango Sambal, Plum Sauce, Peanut and Pepper Relish, Cucumber and Carrot Relish

SNACKS, APPETIZERS, AND SOUPS

Outdoor stalls all over the countries of the Far East sell all kinds of "fast food," which may be eaten sitting at nearby wooden benches, or while walking along the street. A selection of these Asian "snacks" can make an original first course for any meal, either Asian- or Western-style. They also make perfect finger-food for cocktail parties or buffets. Soups are just as popular in the Far East as they are here. They are not usually served at the beginning of a meal, however, but are generally brought to the table with all the other dishes and are dipped into throughout the meal. Nevertheless, most Asian soups do adapt perfectly to Western eating habits and make ideal first courses or light lunch or supper dishes.

Clockwise from the left: Potsticker Dumplings (page 14), Little Barbecued Pork Turnovers (page 21), and Sesame Shrimp Toasts (page 14)

POTSTICKER
DUMPLINGS *are a*
popular Chinese
snack often included
in the "dim sum"
menus traditional to
family Sunday
brunches, which
feature dumplings of
all types – steamed,
grilled, and fried.

SESAME SHRIMP TOASTS

MAKES 24

½ lb raw shrimp in their shells
2 heaping tbsp canned Chinese water chestnuts, drained
2 bacon slices, chopped
½ tsp salt
1 tsp cornstarch
white of 1 medium egg
6 slices of white bread, crusts removed
¼ cup sesame seeds
vegetable oil, for frying

Remove the shells from the shrimp. Using a sharp knife, make an incision along the length of the back of each shrimp (the outside curve). Remove and discard any dark vein.

Place the shrimp, water chestnuts, bacon, salt, cornstarch, and egg white in the bowl of a blender or food processor and reduce to a smooth purée.

Alternatively, reduce the ingredients to a purée in a large mortar with a pestle, or simply mince them as fine as possible with a sharp knife.

Spread the purée evenly over the slices of bread.

Spread an even layer of sesame seeds on a large plate and then press in the spread sides of the bread to coat the tops evenly with seeds.

Fill a frying pan or wok with oil to a depth of about 1 inch. Heat until nice and hot, then fry the toasts, coated-side down, until the seeds are crisp and golden, 1 minute or so. Turn and fry on the other side until the bread is crisp and golden. Drain on paper towels.

Cut each slice into 4 even strips and serve as soon as possible.

POTSTICKER DUMPLINGS

MAKES 16

1 ¼ cups flour
2 tbsp vegetable oil
⅔ cup chicken or vegetable stock
Asian sweet chili sauce or other dipping sauce, for
serving
FOR THE FILLING
¾ cup flaked white crab meat
3 tbsp minced green cabbage
1 small scallion, minced
1-inch cube of peeled fresh gingerroot, minced
1 tbsp dry sherry
1 tbsp soy sauce
¼ tsp salt
1 tsp Asian sesame oil
¼ tsp sugar

In a bowl, mix the flour with ½ cup of very hot water to make a dough. Knead 10 minutes, adding a little more water if the dough seems too dry or a little more flour if it seems too sticky. Cover with a damp cloth and let rest 30 minutes.

Meanwhile, make the filling: Mix all the ingredients together in a bowl.

Knead the rested dough 5 minutes longer and then divide it into 16 equal balls. On a floured surface, roll out the balls to make rounds of dough with a diameter of about 3 inches. Keep the balls and rounds of dough covered with a damp cloth while working to prevent their drying out.

Place a small teaspoon of stuffing in the center of each round. Moisten the edges with water. Fold each over in half to make a half-moon and pinch the edges to seal. Using thumb and forefinger, "frill" the edges to make each dumpling into a small pasty shape, with a frilly seam on top and a flat base.

Heat the oil in a frying or sauté pan that is large enough to take the dumplings snugly in one layer and that preferably has a tight-fitting lid. Fry the dumplings over very low heat until their flat bottoms are crisp and golden.

Pour in the stock, cover, and simmer over very low heat until all the liquid has been absorbed, 12–15 minutes. Remove the lid and cook 2 minutes longer.

Serve hot, accompanied by sweet chili sauce or another dipping sauce.

THAI FISH CAKES

MAKES 8

½ lb skinless white fish fillets, coarsely chopped
1 ½ tsp Thai red curry paste
1 tbsp cornstarch
1 tbsp fish sauce
1 medium egg, beaten
1 large hot red or green chili pepper, seeded and chopped
2 shallots, minced
3 oz green beans, minced
2 tbsp vegetable oil
Cucumber and Carrot Relish (see page 10) or a dipping sauce, for serving

In a blender or food processor, blend the fish until just smooth. Add the curry paste, cornstarch, fish sauce, and egg and process briefly until mixed. Be careful not to over-process, or the fish will lose all texture! Transfer to a small bowl and mix in the chili pepper, shallots, and beans.

Divide the mixture into 8 portions and shape them into round cakes about ¼-inch thick.

Heat the oil in a frying pan over medium heat and fry the cakes until uniformly golden, 3–4 minutes on each side.

Serve immediately, with Cucumber and Carrot Relish or a dipping sauce.

DEEP-FRIED "SEAWEED"

SERVES 4

½ lb cabbage or collard greens, very finely shredded
vegetable oil, for deep-frying
sugar, for sprinkling

Heat the oil in a wok until just beginning to smoke, then deep-fry the cabbage, in small batches, for a few seconds only, until it turns dark and crispy.

Remove each batch with a slotted spoon, drain on paper towels, and keep warm while the remaining batches are being cooked. Sprinkle with a little sugar as soon as all the greens are cooked and serve.

THAI RED CURRY PASTE *is flavored with lime zest, lemongrass, galangal, and trassi – the Southeast Asian condiment made from fermented shrimp – and is available from Asian markets.*

As here, the DEEP-FRIED "SEAWEED" *served in many Chinese restaurants is not seaweed at all but shredded greens. Use a food processor to shred them very finely.*

Popular in Singapore, Malaysia, and Indonesia, SATAY dishes consist of tiny "kebabs" and may contain meat, poultry, or fish.

Japanese TERIYAKI SAUCE, made from soybeans and wine and used as a marinade and basting sauce, is available bottled from Asian markets, as are small wooden skewers.

CHICKEN SATAY

MAKES 8 SMALL SKEWERS

½ lb skinless boneless chicken breast, cut into
¾-inch cubes
FOR THE MARINADE
1 tbsp brown sugar
2 tbsp soy sauce
juice of ½ lemon
1 tbsp vegetable oil
FOR THE DIPPING SAUCE
1 tbsp vegetable oil
1 small onion, minced
1 garlic clove, minced
1 tbsp crunchy peanut butter
1 tbsp Asian sweet chili sauce
1 tsp soy sauce
3 tbsp boiling water

First make the marinade: In a small bowl, dissolve the sugar in 1 tablespoon of hot water and then add the remaining ingredients and mix well. Add the chicken pieces and stir until well coated, then let marinate at least 1 hour, or up to 24 hours in the refrigerator.

Meanwhile make the dipping sauce: In a small pan, heat the oil over medium heat and cook the onion until softened. Then add the remaining ingredients and simmer 3 minutes. Transfer to a serving bowl and let cool.

Soak 8 small wooden skewers in water for 30 minutes or more, to prevent their scorching too much during cooking. Preheat the broiler, a grill, or barbecue.

Thread the marinated meat on the prepared skewers and cook them under the broiler or on the grill or barbecue for 4–5 minutes, turning once.

Serve accompanied by the dipping sauce.

Note: For an unusual and attractive presentation, use bay twigs instead of skewers.

TERIYAKI CHICKEN

MAKES 12 SKEWERS

2 tbsp vegetable oil
⅓ cup teriyaki sauce
1 tbsp dry sherry
1 tbsp brown sugar
1 garlic clove, minced
1-inch cube of peeled fresh gingerroot, crushed in a
garlic press or minced
½ small red sweet pepper, seeded and cut into
½-inch squares
½ lb skinless boneless chicken breast, cut into
½-inch cubes
strips of scallion and cucumber, for serving

Soak 12 small wooden skewers in water for 30 minutes or more, to prevent their scorching too much during grilling.

Place all the ingredients except the chicken, scallion, and cucumber in a bowl and mix them well to combine.

Drop the pieces of chicken into the marinade and toss them well to ensure that they are coated on all sides. Cover and let marinate at least 30 minutes, or up to 3 hours, shaking the bowl occasionally.

Preheat the broiler, a grill, or barbecue.

Thread the pieces of chicken and red pepper on the skewers and grill or barbecue for about 5 minutes, or until cooked through, turning 2 or 3 times and brushing each time with marinade.

Serve immediately, accompanied by the scallion and cucumber.

Clockwise from the bottom left: Teriyaki Chicken, Chicken Satay, and Water Chestnuts in Crispy Bacon (page 20)

THAI STUFFED CHICKEN WINGS

MAKES 12

12 chicken wing portions (see below)
¼ lb ground pork
⅓ cup canned bamboo shoots, drained
⅓ cup canned Chinese water chestnuts, drained
1 oz button mushrooms
2 garlic cloves, minced
2 tsp dark soy sauce
1 tsp sugar
salt and freshly ground black pepper
1 egg, lightly beaten
¼ cup flour
vegetable oil, for deep-frying and greasing
Plum Sauce (see page 10), for serving

Buy whole wing portions: Two sections plus the wing tip. Sever the joint between the two sections. Skin and bone the meatiest section. Grind the meat and add it to the pork in a large bowl.

Mince the bamboo shoots, water chestnuts, and mushrooms in a food processor and add to the meat mixture, together with the garlic, soy sauce, sugar, and a good seasoning of salt and pepper. Mix well together, add the egg to bind and mix well again.

Using a small, sharp-pointed knife, bone the second section of the wings, working from the cut end. There are two bones, one bigger than the other, which will be joined together at that cut end. Separate them first with the point of the knife. The bigger bone will also be firmly attached to the meat on the side opposite to the small bone – carefully detach this with the knife.

Now using the edge of the knife, scrape the meat downward from the bones, being careful not to cut

Top: Sesame Beef Balls; bottom: Thai Stuffed Chicken Wings

the skin. Work down to the joint, then twist and snap off each bone in turn. Discard these bones or reserve them for stock. This will leave wing tips with a hollow pocket of skin and meat attached.

Using a teaspoon and your fingers, fill the cavities with the meat mixture. They should be filled until they are almost overflowing.

Place the stuffed wings in the lightly oiled upper part of a steamer and steam over boiling water until firm, about 20 minutes. Let cool.

Season the flour with salt and pepper. Coat the cooled wings in it and deep-fry them in batches in hot oil in a wok until the skin is golden brown and crisp. Drain on paper towels and keep warm while the rest are being cooked.

Serve immediately, with Plum Sauce.

SESAME BEEF BALLS

SERVES 4

¾ lb ground round steak
3 bacon slices, chopped
1 tbsp chopped celery
1 tbsp chopped carrot
1 tbsp minced mushroom
2 scallions, chopped
1 tbsp cornstarch
1 tbsp soy sauce
1 tbsp dry sherry
½ tsp salt
freshly ground black pepper
flour, for dusting
1 egg, beaten
vegetable oil, for deep-frying
2 tbsp hoisin sauce
2 tsp sugar
1 tbsp sesame seeds
hoisin sauce, Plum Sauce (see page 10), or other
dipping sauce, for serving

Put the beef, bacon, chopped vegetables, mushrooms, scallions, cornstarch, two-thirds of the soy sauce, the sherry, salt, and some pepper in a blender or food processor and process until well mixed. Be careful not to over-process.

Using floured hands, form the paste into walnut-sized balls. Coat these thoroughly and evenly in the beaten egg.

Deep-fry the coated balls in hot oil in a wok until well browned all over. Drain the cooked balls on paper towels.

Remove all but 2 tablespoons of the oil from the wok and add the remaining soy sauce, the hoisin sauce, sugar, and sesame seeds.

Heat the wok over medium heat. Add the beef balls and cook a few minutes, shaking the wok occasionally, until the balls are coated with the sauces and sesame seeds and turn a deep mahogany brown all over.

Serve immediately, with more hoisin sauce, Plum Sauce, or other dipping sauce.

Fresh CHINESE
WATER CHESTNUTS
are occasionally
available from
Chinese markets.

HOISIN SAUCE, *one*
of the most popular
dipping sauces in
China, is available
in bottles from most
supermarkets.

EGG-ROLL *wrappers are available fresh or frozen from Asian markets and many supermarkets, as are* CHINESE DRIED MUSHROOMS.

ASIAN SESAME OIL, *made from toasted sesame seeds, is aromatic and flavorful.*

WATER CHESTNUTS IN CRISPY BACON

SERVES 4

about ½ lb sliced bacon
1¼ cups canned Chinese water chestnuts, drained

Soak some wooden toothpicks in water for 30 minutes or more to prevent them from burning during cooking. Preheat the broiler, a grill, or barbecue.

Using the back of a knife, scrape each slice of bacon to stretch it a little and then cut it crosswise in half.

Wrap each water chestnut in a piece of bacon and secure with a toothpick.

Broil or grill, turning once, until the bacon is crisp, 5–7 minutes.

Serve immediately.

SPRING ROLLS

MAKES 12

12 spring roll wrappers
vegetable oil, for deep-frying
FOR THE FILLING
5 dried Chinese mushrooms
1 tbsp vegetable oil
½ tsp Asian sesame oil
½ lb ground pork
2 scallions, minced
2 garlic cloves, minced
1 small carrot, grated
6 canned Chinese water chestnuts, drained and chopped
2½ oz peeled cooked shrimp, chopped
1 tbsp soy sauce
1 egg, beaten

Soak the dried mushrooms in warm water for 30 minutes. Drain, remove and discard the stems, and slice the caps thinly.

Make the filling: Heat the oils in a wok or frying pan over medium heat and stir-fry the pork 5 minutes. Add the scallions, garlic, carrot, mushrooms, and water chestnuts and stir-fry 2 minutes longer. Let the mixture cool.

Add the shrimp, soy sauce, and most of the egg, saving a little egg to seal the wrappers.

Divide the mixture into 12 portions and place one on the edge of each egg-roll wrapper. Fold in the sides of each and roll it up, brushing the seam with a little of the reserved egg to seal.

Deep-fry the rolls, in batches, in hot oil in a wok until golden and crisp, 4–5 minutes. Be careful not to have the oil too hot or the wrappers will burn before the filling is cooked through. Drain on paper towels and keep warm while the rest are being cooked. Serve as soon as all are cooked.

NOTE: Serve with a dipping sauce made from equal parts soy sauce and rice or wine vinegar.

LITTLE BARBECUED PORK TURNOVERS

MAKES 16

2 oz Chinese barbecued pork (see below), minced
1 tbsp vegetable oil
½ cup minced scallions
2 tsp oyster sauce
1 tsp dark soy sauce
1 tsp sugar
½ tsp salt
3 tbsp cornstarch
¼ cup chicken stock
1 egg yolk
1 tbsp milk
2 tbsp sesame seeds
Asian sweet chili sauce or other dipping sauce, for serving

FOR THE PASTRY

¾ cup flour
pinch of salt
4 tbsp butter, cut into small pieces

Barbecued pork is available from Chinese restaurants and markets.

Preheat the oven to 425°F.

First make the pastry: In a bowl, mix the flour and salt and then rub in the butter until the mixture resembles fine bread crumbs. Add just enough cold water to form a dough. Knead well and chill 30 minutes.

Meanwhile, make the filling: Heat the oil in a wok over low heat and soften the scallions briefly. Mix them with the pork, sauces, sugar, and salt in a small saucepan.

Mix the cornstarch to a paste with a little of the stock, then add the remaining stock. Mix this into the contents of the pan. Bring to a boil and simmer over low heat, stirring constantly, until thickened. Let the mixture cool completely.

Roll out the pastry dough very thinly and cut out sixteen 3-inch rounds, re-rolling the trimmings as necessary.

Put a teaspoon of filling in the center of each round. Slightly dampen the edges of each round with a very little water and fold in half to form little half-moon shapes. Pinch the edges together well to seal them and arrange the turnovers on a baking sheet.

Mix the egg yolk and milk and brush the turnovers with a little of this egg wash. Sprinkle them with sesame seeds and bake until crisp and golden brown, about 15 minutes.

Serve immediately, accompanied by sweet chili sauce or another dipping sauce.

OYSTER SAUCE, although made from oysters, does not taste fishy but is used to give depth of flavor to a wide variety of dishes and is available in bottles from Asian markets and large supermarkets. Several varieties of chili sauce are also available. The ASIAN SWEET CHILI SAUCE called for in recipes here is smooth and thick, and is sweetened with sugar or fruit.

MICHAEL'S THAI BEEF SOUP

SERVES 4

*The recipe for this
delicious main-course
soup was given to
me by the chef at
my local Thai
restaurant.
FRESH CILANTRO
leaves are often sold
complete with their
stems and roots,
which make useful
flavorings. STAR
ANISE is a pungent
star-shaped spice
with a strong
aniseed flavor.*

8 garlic cloves
1 ½ lb piece of beef chuck
¼ cup chopped cilantro root and stem (see left)
6 star anise
2 carrots, chopped
2 celery stalks, chopped
1 onion, chopped
2 tbsp soy sauce
1 beef bouillon cube
1 tbsp brown sugar
2 tsp salt
¾ lb Chinese noodles
½ lb fresh bean sprouts (about 2 cups)
vegetable oil, for deep-frying
about 4 tbsp fish sauce
about ¼ tsp chili powder
2 scallions, chopped
fresh cilantro leaves, for garnish

Coarsely chop 4 garlic cloves and slice the rest.

Put the beef in a large pan with the chopped garlic, cilantro, star anise, carrots, celery, onion, soy sauce, bouillon cube, sugar, salt, and 7 cups of water. Bring to a boil and simmer 40 minutes.

Remove the meat from the stock and let it cool slightly. When cool enough to handle, cut it into thin, bite-sized pieces and keep these warm.

Cook the noodles according to the package directions. Blanch the bean sprouts in boiling salted water 1 minute only. Deep-fry the garlic slices in hot oil in a wok or small pan until golden. Drain.

Strain the soup into a clean pan, reheat, and add fish sauce and chili powder to taste.

Put the bean sprouts in 4 warmed soup bowls. Arrange the noodles, meat, and scallions on top.

Ladle in the soup and garnish with the garlic and cilantro leaves. Serve with spoons and forks.

The flavor of THAI SHRIMP SOUP *relies on fragrant* LEMON-GRASS *and* KAFFIR LIME LEAVES, *which add a strong citrus note without acidity. These are available, fresh or dried, from Asian markets. Lemon or lime zest can be used instead, but will not give the same distinctive taste.* GALANGAL, *a spice related to ginger, is available from Asian markets. Fresh gingerroot can be substituted.*

QUICK CHICKEN AND COCONUT SOUP

SERVES 4

2 cups chicken stock
grated zest of ½ washed lime
juice of 1 ½ limes
3 tbsp fish sauce
1 tsp ground ginger
½ tsp chili powder
1 ¼ cups thick canned coconut milk
6 oz skinless boneless chicken breast, cut across in thin slices
chopped fresh cilantro, for garnish
sliced hot chili peppers, for garnish (optional)

Put the stock in a saucepan with the lime zest and juice, the fish sauce, ginger, and chili powder and simmer 5 minutes.

Add the coconut milk and chicken slices and simmer until the chicken is just cooked through, 2–3 minutes longer.

Pour into 4 warmed bowls and garnish with cilantro and chili slices, if using.

THAI SHRIMP SOUP

SERVES 4

¾ lb raw medium shrimp in their shells
3 hot chili peppers
1 tbsp vegetable oil
2 stalks of lemongrass, thinly sliced
3 Kaffir lime leaves
3 slices of galangal, each about ½-inch thick
2 garlic cloves, chopped
2 tbsp fish sauce, or more to taste
juice of ½ lime
1 tbsp chopped fresh cilantro, for garnish
3 chopped scallions, for garnish

Remove the shells from the shrimp; put the shrimp to one side and reserve the shells. Seed the chili peppers. Coarsely chop 2 of them and thinly slice the third into rings.

Heat the oil in a saucepan over medium heat and fry the shrimp shells until they turn pink, 1–2 minutes.

Add 1½ quarts of water, the coarsely chopped chili peppers, the lemongrass, Kaffir lime leaves, galangal, garlic, and fish sauce. Bring to a boil, then reduce the heat, and simmer 20 minutes. Strain into a clean pan and discard the solids.

Add the shrimp and cook until they become pink and opaque, 3–4 minutes. Do not overcook or the shrimp will be tough and tasteless.

Add the lime juice and, if the soup seems too bland, add a little more fish sauce to taste.

Pour into 4 warmed bowls and garnish with the rings of chili pepper, the cilantro and the chopped scallions.

CORN AND CRAB SOUP★

SERVES 4

3 ½ cups chicken stock
½-inch cube of peeled fresh gingerroot, crushed through
a garlic press or minced
1 tsp soy sauce
1 tsp sugar
1 ½ cups canned or frozen whole-kernel corn, drained or
thawed
1 tbsp cornstarch
3 tbsp dry sherry
1 ½ cups flaked crab meat
1 egg white, lightly beaten
(★see page 2 for advice on eggs)
1 tsp Asian sesame oil
6 tbsp chopped cooked ham, for garnish (optional)
1 thinly sliced scallion, for garnish

Put the chicken stock in a saucepan with the ginger, soy sauce, sugar, and corn. Bring to a boil, then reduce the heat and simmer 2–3 minutes.

In a small bowl, mix the cornstarch with the sherry. Remove the pan from the heat and whisk the cornstarch mixture into the soup. Simmer until the soup thickens, about 2 minutes longer.

Add the crab meat and cook another minute or so to warm it through.

Remove the soup from the heat once more. Whisk the egg white with the sesame oil and then vigorously whisk this into the soup so that it forms white strands.

Pour into 4 warmed bowls and sprinkle with chopped ham, if using, and the sliced scallion.

HOT AND SOUR SOUP

SERVES 4

4 dried Chinese mushrooms
5 cups chicken stock
¼ lb skinless boneless chicken breast, cut in thin slivers
3 oz peeled cooked small shrimp
4 oz tofu, cut into ½-inch cubes
¼ cup chopped canned bamboo shoots, drained
½ cup frozen peas
2 scallions, chopped
2 tbsp soy sauce
3 tbsp rice or white wine vinegar
2 tbsp cornstarch
salt and freshly ground black pepper
1 tsp Asian sesame oil, for serving

Soak the dried mushrooms in warm water for 30 minutes. Drain them, remove and discard the stems, and slice the caps thinly.

Bring the stock to a boil in a saucepan, add the mushrooms and chicken, and simmer 10 minutes.

Add the shrimp, tofu, bamboo shoots, peas, and scallions and simmer 2 more minutes.

In a bowl, mix together the soy sauce, vinegar, cornstarch, and 6 tablespoons of water. Season with salt and plenty of pepper to give the soup its characteristic "hot" flavor.

Stir this mixture into the soup and simmer until the soup thickens, about 2 minutes longer.

Pour the soup into warmed bowls and add a few drops of sesame oil to each before serving.

A wide variety of bottled FISH SAUCES *is made from fermented fish by various Asian countries. This salty condiment, used as a flavor-enhancer and not just in fish dishes, is available from Asian supermarkets.*

TOFU, *or soybean curd, is available from most supermarkets and health-food stores as well as Asian markets.*

MAIN-COURSE DISHES

T he Asian style of eating is quite different from our traditional Western concept of main courses. Instead, an Asian meal will usually consist of a central dish of rice or noodles accompanied by a variety of "made" dishes. These might be only a couple of stir-fries for a simple family meal, or there could be a succession of countless elaborate recipes for a banquet or special occasion. Whatever the type of meal, however, the balance of ingredients will invariably tip

heavily toward fresh vegetables, grains, and fruit, with meat, poultry, and fish appearing in much smaller quantities than is generally the case in the West. For this reason alone, the Asian diet is a very healthy one.

Many of the dishes in this chapter can be served as Western-style main courses with accompanying rice and vegetables.

Dover Sole with Mushrooms and Pork (page 28) served with steamed white rice

Sesame-Crusted Salmon with Ginger Cream is a particularly fine East-meets-West recipe that provides a simple and different way of cooking salmon to bring out its delicate flavor.

Dried Chinese black mushrooms are very similar to dried French cèpes and Italian porcini.

SESAME-CRUSTED SALMON WITH GINGER CREAM

SERVES 4

⅓ cup sesame seeds
1 egg, beaten
flour, for coating
4 skinless pieces of salmon fillet, each weighing 4–5 oz
salt and freshly ground black pepper
3 tbsp vegetable oil
FOR THE SAUCE
1¼ cups light cream
1½-inch cube of peeled fresh gingerroot, crushed
through a garlic press
1 tbsp light soy sauce or more to taste

Toast the sesame seeds in a frying pan over low to medium heat until lightly colored and aromatic. Put the toasted sesame seeds, beaten egg, and some flour in 3 separate shallow dishes.

Season the fish fillets on both sides with salt and pepper. Dip them first in the flour, shaking off the excess, then dip them in the egg, and finally in the toasted sesame seeds.

Heat the oil in a frying pan over medium-low heat and fry the coated fish until crisp and golden and cooked through, 2–3 minutes on each side.

Meanwhile, make the sauce: Combine the cream, ginger, and soy sauce in a small pan and simmer 2–3 minutes. Add a little more soy sauce to taste.

Serve accompanied by steamed white rice or noodles and fresh steamed or boiled vegetables.

DOVER SOLE WITH MUSHROOMS AND PORK

SERVES 4

1½ oz dried Chinese black mushrooms
1 whole Dover sole, weighing about 1 lb 2 oz, skinned
1 tsp cornstarch
2 tsp dry sherry
½ tsp Asian sesame oil, plus more for greasing
¼ tsp soy sauce
1 tsp oyster sauce
1½ oz lean boneless pork, shredded
1 slice of bacon, cut crosswise into thin strips
½-inch cube of peeled fresh gingerroot, cut into fine
matchsticks
1 small scallion, thinly sliced, for garnish
chopped fresh cilantro, for garnish

Soak the mushrooms in warm water for 30 minutes. Drain them thoroughly, cut off and discard the stems, and thinly slice the caps.

Arrange the fish in a steamer. (First put 2 strips of lightly oiled foil in a cross shape in the bottom of the pan: This will make it easier to remove the fish when it is cooked.)

Blend the cornstarch with a little of the sherry, then mix this thoroughly with the remaining sherry, the sesame oil, soy and oyster sauces, pork, bacon, and ginger.

Spoon this mixture on top of the fish and steam it over boiling water until the flesh flakes readily, 10–15 minutes.

Transfer the fish to a warmed serving plate and garnish with the scallion and cilantro.

CHILI SHRIMP IN PINEAPPLES

SERVES 4

2 small, ripe pineapples
1 tbsp vegetable oil
1 onion, chopped
1 garlic clove, minced
1 large or 2 small celery stalks, coarsely chopped
2 tbsp chopped sweet pepper (preferably red)
1 tsp chili powder or more to taste
salt and freshly ground black pepper
1 cup chicken stock
2 heaping tsp arrowroot, mixed with a little water
¾ lb peeled cooked small or medium shrimp
1 cup small seedless grapes (any color or mixed)
½ cup blanched split almonds, toasted, for garnish
4 large or 8 medium cooked shrimp in their shells, for garnish

Cut the pineapples in half lengthwise, including the crown of green leaves. Being careful not to cut through the skin, cut out all the flesh and set the shells aside in a warm place. Cut the flesh into bite-sized pieces, discarding any hard core, and set the flesh aside.

Heat the oil in a large saucepan and cook the onion until translucent. Add the garlic, celery, sweet pepper, and chili powder with salt and pepper to taste. Stir-fry until the vegetables are softened, 2–3 minutes.

Stir in the stock, bring to a boil, and simmer 15 minutes. Add the arrowroot mixture and stir well until the mixture has thickened.

Add the peeled shrimp, grapes, and pineapple pieces and continue to cook gently until these are just heated through. (The shrimp will toughen if cooked too long.)

Pile the cooked shrimp mixture into the reserved pineapple half shells and garnish with toasted almonds and the shrimp in shells.

For a striking buffet party dish, serve the CHILI SHRIMP IN PINEAPPLE *in one or two half shells from a large pineapple. A wide variety of seafood suits this treatment: Try using scallops or crab meat.*

SPICED CRAB CLAWS

SERVES 4

2 tbsp vegetable oil
8 large or 12 medium shelled crab claws, thawed if frozen
1 small onion, minced
2 garlic cloves, minced
2 hot chili peppers, minced
1½-inch cube of peeled fresh gingerroot, minced
½ tsp ground coriander seeds
1 tsp sugar
1 tbsp soy sauce
2 tsp tomato paste
salt
juice of ½ lime

In a frying pan or wok, heat the oil over medium heat and fry the crab claws until cooked through, 3–4 minutes. Remove with a slotted spoon and keep warm.

In the oil remaining in the pan, fry the onion, garlic, and chili 3 minutes. Add the ginger, coriander, sugar, soy cause, tomato paste, and salt to taste with 3 tablespoons of water and simmer 3 minutes.

Return the crab claws to the pan. Add the lime juice, stir to coat thoroughly, and simmer 1–2 minutes, stirring until piping hot.

Shelled crab claws can be bought frozen from Asian markets.

MALAYSIAN MILD CURRY PASTE *is sold in many specialty markets. If unavailable, substitute another strong curry paste or a mild Malaysian curry powder.*

MUSSELS WITH CURRIED COCONUT NOODLES

SERVES 4

2¼ lb cleaned and debearded mussels in their shells
1¼ cups canned coconut cream
7 oz jar Malaysian mild curry paste
½ lb Chinese noodles
curls of fresh coconut, peeled with a swivel-bladed vegetable peeler, for garnish
chopped fresh cilantro, for garnish (optional)

Soak the mussels in cold water at least 1 hour to remove any traces of dirt or sand, changing the water at least 3 times. Drain the mussels and give any that remain open a sharp tap. Those that do not close again are dead and must be thrown away.

Put the coconut cream and the curry paste in a large saucepan that has a tight-fitting lid and place over medium heat, stirring gently. Add the mussels, cover the pan, and cook about 5 minutes, shaking the pan occasionally, until all the shells have opened. (Those few that do not should also be discarded.) Do not overcook or the mussels will be tough and rubbery.

Meanwhile, cook the noodles in boiling water, according to the package directions, and then drain them thoroughly.

To serve: Divide the noodles among 6 warmed bowls or dishes and pour the mussels and sauce over them. Sprinkle with coconut curls and chopped cilantro, if using, and serve immediately.

Top: Mussels with Curried Coconut Noodles; bottom: Spiced Crab Claws

For the CRISPY SESAME SHRIMP, *it is important to keep the tails attached to the shrimp when peeling them. They then look much more attractive when cooked and are easier to dip in the sauce and eat.*

CRISPY SESAME SHRIMP

SERVES 4

½ lb large raw shrimp, peeled and deveined
vegetable oil, for deep-frying
Asian sweet chili sauce or other dipping sauce, for
serving

FOR THE BATTER

⅔ cup flour
3 tbsp cornstarch
1 tsp baking powder
¼ tsp chili powder
½ tsp salt
1 tbsp vegetable oil
2 tbsp sesame seeds

At least 1 hour ahead, make the batter: Thoroughly mix the flour, cornstarch, baking powder, and chili powder with ¾ cup water in a bowl. Let the batter rest at least 1 hour.

Just before using, beat the salt and oil into the batter until well incorporated and then stir in the sesame seeds.

Dip the shrimp in the batter and deep-fry them, a few at a time, in hot oil in a wok. Drain on paper towels and keep warm while the rest are being cooked.

Serve as soon as all the shrimp are cooked, accompanied by a dipping sauce, such as sweet chili sauce or a mixture of equal parts light soy sauce and rice or white wine vinegar.

Top: Sesame-Crusted Salmon with Ginger Cream (page 28);
bottom: Crispy Sesame Shrimp

INDONESIAN SQUID

SERVES 4

1 tbsp vegetable oil
1 small onion, chopped
2 garlic cloves, minced
1-inch cube of peeled fresh gingerroot, minced
½ tsp chili powder
grated zest and juice of 1 washed lime
1 tbsp brown sugar
1¾ cups thick canned coconut milk
12 small prepared squid, sacs sliced into thin rings
salt
chopped fresh cilantro, for garnish

Heat the oil in a saucepan or wok over medium heat and fry the onion, garlic, and ginger 2–3 minutes.

Add the chili powder, lime zest and juice, the sugar, and salt to taste. Stir to mix well, then add the coconut milk. Simmer 10 minutes.

Add the squid tentacles and slices and simmer 10 minutes. Do not overcook or it will become tough and rubbery. Serve sprinkled with chopped cilantro.

Prepared SQUID are available fresh from better fishmongers and frozen from Asian markets.

CRISPY DUCK WITH PANCAKES

SERVES 4–6

1 duck, weighing 4–4 ½ lb giblets removed
salt
24 small Chinese pancakes (Beijing doilies)
hoisin sauce, for serving
4 scallions, cut into small shreds, for serving
¼ English cucumber, cut into small sticks, for serving

At least 6 hours ahead, pour a large kettle of boiling water over the duck. This will tighten the skin. Then dry the bird thoroughly inside and out, place it on a rack, and let dry in an airy place at least 6 hours, but preferably up to 12.

Preheat the oven to 350°F.

Prick the skin of the duck all over with a skewer to let the fat escape during cooking, then rub the skin all over with salt.

Place the bird on a rack in a roasting pan and roast 2 hours. The meat will become very tender and the skin very crisp.

To serve: Pull the meat off the carcass and shred this and the skin by pulling it apart with two forks. Arrange the meat and skin on a warmed serving platter and keep warm.

Warm the pancakes for a couple of minutes in a steamer and then serve these on a warmed serving plate. Serve the sauce, scallions, and cucumber in separate bowls.

Each pancake is spread with a little sauce. A few pieces of scallion and cucumber are then arranged on top of this, followed by some of the duck meat and some of the crispy skin. The pancake is then rolled up and eaten with the fingers. Be sure to provide plenty of napkins and finger-bowls.

CHINESE PANCAKES *for this well-loved dish are available in packages from Chinese markets.*

The recipe for
BALINESE-STYLE
DUCK *was given to
me by a dance
teacher in whose
house I stayed on
Bali. I have had to
adapt it slightly, as
not all the spices
used are available
in the West.*

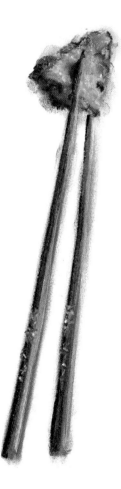

BALINESE-STYLE DUCK

SERVES 6

1 duck, weighing 4–4½ lb, with giblets
1½ tsp salt
½ tsp chili powder
½ tsp ground cumin
½ tsp ground coriander
6 hard-cooked eggs, quartered, for serving
deep-fried onion rings, for garnish (optional)

FOR THE SAUCE
1 tbsp vegetable oil
1 small onion, chopped
1 garlic clove, minced
1-inch cube of peeled fresh gingerroot, crushed through a
garlic press or minced
1 hot chili pepper, seeded and chopped
grated zest and juice of 1 washed lemon
2 tsp brown sugar
1¼ cups canned coconut cream
2 tsp soy sauce

At least 6 hours ahead, remove the giblets from the duck and set them aside. Pour a large kettle of boiling water over the duck. This will tighten the skin. Then dry the bird thoroughly inside and out, place it on a rack, and let dry in an airy place at least 6 hours, but preferably up to 12.

Put the giblets in a small pan, add just enough water to cover, and bring to a boil, skimming off any scum that rises to the surface. Cover and simmer 1 hour. Discard the giblets and boil the stock hard until reduced to about 2 tablespoons. Set aside. Preheat the oven to 350°F.

Prick the skin of the duck all over with a skewer to let the fat escape during cooking. Mix 1 teaspoon of the salt with the chili powder, cumin, and coriander and rub this all over the skin. Place the bird on a rack in a roasting pan and roast 2 hours. The skin will become crisp and golden.

Toward the end of this time, make the sauce: Heat the oil in a pan over medium heat and cook the onion until translucent. Add the reduced stock with the garlic, ginger, chili, lemon zest and juice, sugar, coconut cream, soy sauce, and remaining salt. Bring to a boil, cover, and simmer 30 minutes.

When the duck is cooked, remove from the oven and let it rest 10 minutes. Remove all the skin, cut it into bite-sized pieces, and set aside.

Remove the meat and cut into bite-sized pieces. Toss in the sauce to coat throughly.

Transfer to a warmed serving dish, surround with the egg quarters, sprinkle over the crispy skin pieces, and garnish with the fried onion rings, if using. Serve with steamed white rice.

JAPANESE DEEP-FRIED CHICKEN

SERVES 4

1 lb skinless boneless chicken breast, cut into 1¼-inch
cubes
cornstarch, for dusting
vegetable oil, for deep-frying
1 green sweet pepper, seeded and cut into strips, for
garnish

FOR THE MARINADE
2 tbsp soy sauce
1 tbsp sake, dry sherry, or white wine
1 garlic clove, minced
juice from a 1¼-inch cube of peeled fresh gingerroot,
crushed through a garlic press

Make the marinade: Mix the ingredients in a bowl. Add the chicken cubes, mix well, and let marinate 1 hour, stirring occasionally.

Drain the chicken thoroughly, discarding the marinade. Toss the pieces of chicken in cornstarch and shake off any excess. Deep-fry them, in batches, in hot oil in a wok until golden brown and crispy, 3–4 minutes. Drain on paper towels and keep each batch warm while cooking the rest.

When all the chicken is cooked, arrange on a warmed serving plate, surround with the pepper strips, and serve immediately.

LEMON CHICKEN

SERVES 4

1 egg white, lightly beaten
3 tsp cornstarch
10 oz skinless boneless chicken breast, cut across into
½-inch strips
vegetable oil, for deep-frying
6 tbsp chicken stock
juice of 1 lemon
2 tsp sugar
2 tsp light soy sauce
2 tsp dry sherry
1 garlic clove, minced
pinch of chili powder
½ small green sweet pepper, seeded and cut into equal
bite-sized pieces

Mix the egg white thoroughly with 2 teaspoons of the cornstarch in a bowl. Then mix in the chicken strips, making sure they are all well coated. Cover and chill 30 minutes.

Deep-fry the chicken in hot oil in a wok for 1 minute, then drain on paper towels. Keep warm.

In a bowl, mix together the stock, lemon juice, sugar, soy sauce, sherry, garlic, and chili powder.

Pour all but 1 tablespoon of oil from the wok and stir-fry the pepper 2 minutes over medium heat. Stir in the stock mixture and simmer 1 minute.

Mix the remaining cornstarch with 1 tablespoon of water, add this to the pan, and simmer 1 more minute, stirring. Return the chicken to the pan and stir-fry about 30 seconds. Serve immediately.

STICKY CHICKEN

SERVES 4

8 chicken wing portions
3 garlic cloves, minced
1½-inch cube of peeled fresh gingerroot, crushed
through a garlic press or minced
juice of 1 lemon
2 tbsp soy sauce
2 tbsp honey
½ tsp chili powder

Divide each chicken wing into pieces by cutting through the joints. Discard the wing tips or use for stock. There should be 16 pieces left.

Combine all the remaining ingredients in a shallow baking dish large enough to accommodate the chicken pieces snugly in 1 layer. Add the chicken and mix to coat thoroughly.

Cover and marinate at least 2 hours in a cool place or up to 24 in the refrigerator.

Preheat the oven to 425°F.

Uncover the dish, turn the chicken pieces once more in the marinade, and put the dish in the oven. Bake 20 minutes, turning and basting halfway through. The chicken will be coated with a delicious sticky glaze.

These pieces of chicken wing are best eaten with the fingers, so supply plenty of napkins and finger-bowls.

SAKE is the rice wine of Japan and is much used in Japanese cooking. Dry sherry makes a good substitute.

Chicken drumsticks or thighs also work well in the STICKY CHICKEN recipe. Increase the cooking time if using these.

CHICKEN WITH STRAW MUSHROOM CURRY

SERVES 4

4 skinless chicken breast halves
2 tbsp vegetable oil
salt and freshly ground black pepper
FOR THE SAUCE
2 tbsp vegetable oil
1 onion, chopped
1 garlic clove, minced
1 stalk of lemongrass, minced
1 hot chili pepper, seeded and chopped
¼ tsp ground cinnamon
½ tsp ground cardamom
1 heaping tsp curry powder
1¼ cups canned coconut cream
15 oz canned straw mushrooms, drained
juice of ½ lemon

If you can't find lemongrass for CHICKEN WITH STRAW MUSHROOM CURRY*, substitute the grated zest of ½ lemon or lime. Small egg-shaped* STRAW MUSHROOMS *are rarely seen fresh in the West, but are readily available canned from Asian markets.*

First make the sauce: Heat the oil in saucepan over medium heat and cook the onion with the garlic and lemongrass, stirring occasionally, until the onion has softened, 4–5 minutes.

Add the chili, dry spices, and curry powder. Stir-fry 1 minute. Add the coconut cream and simmer 5 minutes.

Purée the sauce in a blender or food processor and return it to the pan. Add the mushrooms and simmer until they are warmed through, 2–3 minutes. Stir in the lemon juice and a pinch of salt.

Meanwhile, season the chicken lightly. Heat the oil in a frying pan over medium heat and fry the breast halves gently until golden brown and cooked through, 3–4 minutes on each side.

Arrange the cooked chicken on a warmed serving platter and spoon over the sauce. If serving as part of a meal to be eaten with chopsticks, slice the chicken across into bite-sized pieces.

CHICKEN WITH CASHEW NUTS

SERVES 4

6 oz skinless boneless chicken breast, cut into bite-sized pieces
⅓ cup sliced carrot
2 tbsp vegetable oil
⅓ cup unsalted cashew nuts
3 tbsp sliced canned bamboo shoots
1 tbsp frozen peas
FOR THE MARINADE
2 tbsp cornstarch
1 tsp vegetable oil
FOR THE SAUCE
1 tsp soy sauce
1 tsp dry sherry
½ tsp cornstarch
pinch of salt

First make the marinade: In a small bowl, mix together the cornstarch and oil with 2 tablespoons of water. Add the chicken, mix well, and let marinate 10 minutes.

Blanch the carrot slices in boiling salted water for 2 minutes. Drain.

Heat a wok until it is very hot, then add the oil and stir-fry the chicken until cooked through, 3–4 minutes.

Add the carrot, nuts, bamboo shoots, and peas and stir-fry another minute.

Mix the sauce ingredients together with ¼ cup of water. Add this to the pan and cook another minute or so, until the sauce has thickened. Serve immediately.

Top: Chicken with Straw Mushroom Curry served with cooked noodles; bottom: Chicken with Cashew Nuts

Nuts such as almonds or walnuts can be used instead of cashews in the recipe for CHICKEN WITH CASHEW NUTS.

STUFFED BEAN CURD

MAKES 8

block of firm tofu, weighing about 1½ lb
1 tsp cornstarch, mixed with a little water, plus more
for dusting
3 tbsp vegetable oil
1 cup chicken stock
½ tsp salt
4 tsp Chinese oyster sauce
2 thinly sliced scallions, for garnish
FOR THE STUFFING
¼ lb ground chicken
1 tbsp minced onion
2 tbsp light soy sauce
1½ tsp cornstarch

SPICED BEEF *is also delicious served cold, sliced, as part of a picnic or in sandwiches.*

First make the stuffing by mixing together the ingredients in a bowl.

Cut the tofu into 4 equal portions; they will be about 4-inches square and 1¼-inches thick. Now cut these diagonally across to make triangular wedges. Using a sharp knife, cut a slit into the long side of each wedge and scoop out a little of the tofu to make a pocket to take the stuffing. Be careful not to cut too deeply, and work very carefully as the tofu is fragile.

Dust the inside of each pocket with a little cornstarch and carefully fill with the stuffing.

Heat the oil in a pan wide enough to take the pieces of tofu in one layer (a sauté pan or frying pan is ideal) over very low heat. Place the tofu in the pan, stuffed-side down, and cook until the stuffing is golden brown, about 5 minutes.

Pour in the stock, cover the pan, and simmer 3 minutes. Remove the tofu and keep warm.

Add the salt, oyster sauce, and cornstarch mixture to the pan and simmer until thickened, stirring.

Arrange the tofu on a warmed serving plate, pour over the sauce, and garnish with scallions.

SPICED BEEF

SERVES 4–6

2 tbsp vegetable oil
2 lb boneless beef rump roast or fresh brisket
2 tbsp soy sauce
¼ cup dry sherry
2 garlic cloves, minced
3 star anise
1 tbsp sugar
salt and freshly ground black pepper
3 carrots, thinly sliced
2 tbsp butter
1 tsp Asian sesame oil
2 tsp lemon juice
1 tsp black mustard seeds

Heat the vegetable oil in a saucepan that has a tight-fitting lid and is just large enough to hold the piece of meat snugly. Brown the meat on all sides.

Add the soy sauce, sherry, garlic, and star anise. Cover the pan tightly and cook over very low heat, undisturbed, about 1 hour.

Add the sugar and a good grinding of black pepper, replace the lid, and continue cooking 1 more hour.

Lift the meat out of the pan and let it rest 10 minutes. Meanwhile, boil the liquid in the pan rapidly to reduce it to a sticky sauce.

At the same time, steam the carrots until just tender. Melt the butter with the sesame oil in a saucepan over medium heat and add the lemon juice, mustard seeds, and a pinch of salt. Toss the steamed carrots in this to coat thoroughly.

Cut the meat into slices and arrange them on a warmed serving platter. Drizzle the sauce over and surround the meat with the carrots. Serve accompanied by steamed white rice.

BREADED GINGER STEAKS

SERVES 4

2 boneless steaks, each weighing about 6 oz
1 tbsp soy sauce
1 tbsp dry sherry or white wine
1 garlic clove, minced
1-inch cube of peeled fresh gingerroot, crushed through a
garlic press
flour, for coating
1 egg, beaten
1⅓ cups fine fresh white bread crumbs
3 tbsp vegetable oil
chopped scallions, for garnish

Cut each steak in half to make 4 equal pieces in all. Place these between 2 sheets of plastic wrap, and flatten them with a rolling pin until they are as thin as possible. They should at least double in size.

Mix together the soy sauce, sherry or wine, garlic, and ginger in a wide bowl and then put the flattened steaks into it. Mix well so that all surfaces of the meat are coated. Cover and let marinate in the refrigerator at least 6 hours or up to 24.

Drain the marinated steaks well and pat them dry with paper towels.

Put some flour, the beaten egg, and the bread crumbs in 3 separate shallow dishes. Dip the pieces of steak first in flour and shake off any excess. Then dip them in the beaten egg and finally in the bread crumbs.

Heat the oil in a frying pan (not a wok) over medium-high heat and fry the pieces of steak, in batches if necessary, until the coating is crisp and golden, 1–2 minutes on each side.

Serve Western-style, with plain rice or potatoes and vegetables, or slice the steaks into strips and serve as part of an Asian-style meal. Either way, garnish with chopped scallions.

STIR-FRIED BEEF WITH CELERY

SERVES 4

3 tbsp soy sauce
2 garlic cloves, minced
2 tsp cornstarch
1 tsp sugar
1 lb boneless sirloin steak, cut into thin bite-sized strips
3 tbsp vegetable oil
½ lb celery, cut across at an angle into thin slices
1½-inch cube of peeled fresh gingerroot, thinly sliced

Combine the soy sauce, garlic, cornstarch and sugar in a small bowl. Add the beef strips and mix well until each piece is coated. Let marinate 20–30 minutes.

Heat the oil in a wok or frying pan over medium heat and add the meat mixture. Stir-fry 3–4 minutes.

Add the slices of celery and ginger and continue to stir-fry 4 minutes more. Serve immediately.

Based on a traditional Japanese dish, BREADED GINGER STEAKS is a simple and unusual way to cook steak. It also allows a little expensive meat to go a long way, so it is worth buying the best-quality beef.

SWEET-AND-SOUR SPARERIBS

SERVES 4

3 lb pork spareribs
2 tbsp soy sauce
3 tbsp tomato ketchup
6 tbsp orange juice
2 tbsp white or red wine vinegar
2 tbsp brown sugar
1 tsp salt
2 garlic cloves, minced
1-inch cube of peeled fresh gingerroot, minced
¼ tsp chili powder
freshly ground black pepper

Separate the ribs by cutting down between the bones and put the pieces in a wide baking dish or roasting pan.

Combine the remaining ingredients, season well with pepper, and pour over the ribs. Mix well so that each rib is coated. Cover and let marinate at least 6 hours, or up to 24 in the refrigerator.

Preheat the oven to 350°F.

Bake the ribs, uncovered, for 1½ hours, basting them every 15–20 minutes. Increase the oven to 425°F and cook the ribs 30 minutes longer, turning them over after 15 minutes. The liquid will have almost entirely evaporated, leaving the ribs a deep mahogany brown and covered in a delicious sticky glaze.

These ribs are best eaten with the fingers, so supply lots of napkins and finger-bowls.

Left to right: Stir-Fried Beef with Celery (page 41), Stuffed Bean Curd (page 40), and Sweet-and-Sour Spareribs

PORK WITH NOODLES, MUSHROOMS, AND SPINACH

SERVES 4

¾ lb Chinese noodles
3 tbsp vegetable oil
½ small onion, minced
1-inch cube of peeled fresh gingerroot, minced
2 garlic cloves, minced
2 hot red or green chili peppers, seeded and minced,
plus extra for garnish (optional)
1 lb lean boneless pork, cut into thin bite-sized strips
6 oz firm mushrooms, thinly sliced
salt and freshly ground black pepper
¼ cup white wine or light stock
¾ lb fresh spinach, torn into small shreds

First cook the noodles according to the directions on the package. Drain them well and then toss them in 1 tablespoon of the oil to prevent them from sticking together. Set aside.

Heat the remaining oil in a wok or large saucepan over high heat and stir-fry the onion 1 minute. Add the ginger, garlic, and chili peppers and stir-fry 1 more minute.

Add the pork strips and mushrooms and continue to stir-fry until the meat is cooked and the mushrooms are beginning to soften, 3–4 minutes.

Season with salt and pepper, pour in the wine or stock, and add the spinach. Stir-fry just until the spinach begins to wilt. Do not over-cook: Each piece of spinach should still retain some shape and stay separate rather than sticking together.

Add the noodles to the mixture and continue to stir-fry 1–2 minutes longer, until the ingredients are well mixed and the noodles are really hot.

Serve immediately in 4 warmed bowls and garnish with extra chopped chili peppers, if using.

Note: If fresh spinach is not available, use collard greens or romaine lettuce.

There is a wide variety of very different types of CHINESE NOODLES, *which require varying degrees of cooking. Always check the package for cooking times.*

BALINESE PORK

SERVES 4

2 tbsp vegetable oil
1 lb pork tenderloin, cut into ¾-inch cubes
1 onion, minced
3 garlic cloves, minced
1 hot chili pepper or more to taste, seeded and finely
chopped
1 tsp ground coriander seed
1 tsp turmeric
1 tsp cornstarch
1¼ cups canned coconut cream
1 tsp salt

Heat half the oil in a wok or frying pan that has a tight-fitting lid over medium heat. Stir-fry the pork until the meat is colored all over, 3–4 minutes. Using a slotted spoon, remove the pork from the wok and set aside.

Add the remaining oil to the wok and stir-fry the onion until softened, 3–4 minutes. Add the garlic, chili, coriander, and turmeric and continue to stir-fry 2–3 minutes longer. Return the pork to the wok.

Mix the cornstarch with 1 tablespoon of water and stir this into the coconut cream. Add to the wok and bring to a boil. Add the salt and simmer, covered, over the lowest possible heat until the meat is tender, about 1 hour.

Transfer to a warmed dish to serve.

Pork with Noodles, Mushrooms, and Spinach

VEGETABLES, SALADS, RICE, AND NOODLES

Vegetables in every form feature heavily in all Asian cuisines and are considered important ingredients in their own right, rather than as mere fillers, accompaniments, or garnishes as is so often the case in much of the cooking of the West. Rice and noodles are treated with even greater respect and form the central part of most Asian meals, from breakfast to lavish banquets. These staples are usually served plainly cooked as a perfect bland background for the other more highly fla-vored cooked dishes, but they are occasionally given more elaborate treatment with other ingredients in order to play a more promi-nent starring role in a meal.

Left: Japanese-Style Chicken and Asparagus Salad (page 48); right: Thai Chicken, Shrimp, and Fruit Salad (page 48)

THAI CHICKEN, SHRIMP, AND FRUIT SALAD

SERVES 4 AS A FIRST COURSE

½ mango or papaya, peeled, pitted or seeded, and cut into bite-sized pieces
1 orange, peeled and sectioned
1 small grapefruit, preferably pink, peeled and sectioned
1 pear, peeled, cored, and cut into bite-sized pieces
16 seedless grapes, halved
8 fresh litchis, peeled and seeded
2 tomatoes, cut into small pieces
⅔ cup halved canned Chinese water chestnuts
¾ cup cooked chicken, cut into bite-sized pieces
¼ lb peeled cooked small shrimp
4–6 shallots, thinly sliced
2 garlic cloves, thinly sliced
vegetable oil, for deep frying
2 handfuls mixed salad leaves
¾ cup roughly chopped salted peanuts, for garnish
fresh cilantro sprigs, for garnish (optional)

FOR THE DRESSING
3 tbsp sugar
juice of ½ lime
1 tbsp fish sauce
1 hot red chili pepper, seeded and chopped
1 garlic clove, minced

The classic THAI CHICKEN, SHRIMP AND FRUIT SALAD *makes a spectacular first course or light meal. Any fruit in season can be used; those given here are merely suggestions.*

In a bowl, lightly mix together the fruit, tomatoes, water chestnuts, chicken, and shrimp.

Make the dressing: Dissolve the sugar in ⅓ cup of hot water and let it cool. Then mix in the lime juice, fish sauce, chili, and garlic.

Deep-fry the shallot and garlic slices in hot oil in a wok until crisp. Drain on paper towels.

Just before serving, pour the dressing over the bowl and mix gently. Cover a serving plate with the salad leaves and arrange the salad over this. Scatter over the shallots and garlic, the peanuts, and cilantro, if using, to garnish. Serve immediately.

JAPANESE-STYLE CHICKEN AND ASPARAGUS SALAD

SERVES 4 AS A FIRST COURSE

1 tbsp sake, dry sherry, or white wine
½ tsp salt
about ½ lb skinless boneless chicken breast, cut across into thin slices
1 lb asparagus, cut across at an angle into 1½-inch lengths
salad leaves, for serving (optional)
1 tsp very thin matchstick strips of thinly pared zest from a washed lemon, for garnish

FOR THE DRESSING
1 tsp dry English mustard powder
2 tbsp sake, dry sherry, or white wine
2 tbsp soy sauce

In a small bowl, mix the sake, sherry, or wine with the salt. Toss the chicken slices in this and let marinate 30 minutes.

Bring ⅓ cup of water to a boil in a wok or very small heavy pan. Cook the chicken pieces, stirring constantly, for 1–2 minutes or until just cooked. Using a slotted spoon, transfer the chicken to a bowl and let cool. Reserve the stock left in the wok for making the dressing.

Cook the asparagus in boiling salted water until just tender but still firm, 3–4 minutes. Immediately drain and refresh under cold running water, then drain again. Add to the chicken.

Make the dressing: Mix together the ingredients with 1 tablespoon of the reserved stock.

Just before serving, pour the dressing over the salad and toss well to combine thoroughly. Transfer to a serving plate or dish and serve as part of an Asian-style meal. Alternatively, make 4 individual servings piled on beds of salad leaves, if using, and serve as a Western-style first course. Either way, garnish with the lemon zest.

STIR-FRIED VEGETABLES

SERVES 4 AS AN ACCOMPANIMENT

2 tbsp vegetable oil
1 garlic clove, thinly sliced
1-inch cube of peeled fresh gingerroot, minced
1 hot chili pepper, seeded and chopped (optional)
1 small onion, chopped
1 small carrot, cut across at an angle into slices
½ red, green, or yellow sweet pepper, seeded and cut
into uniform bite-sized pieces
¼ lb sugar peas or snow peas
½ cup canned straw mushrooms, drained
1 tsp cornstarch
1 tbsp soy sauce
chopped scallions, chives, or fresh cilantro, for garnish
(optional)

Heat a wok or large frying pan over medium heat and add the oil. When it is really hot, add the garlic, ginger, and chili, if using, and stir-fry 1 minute.

Add the onion, carrot, and sweet pepper and stir-fry 2–3 minutes longer. Add the sugar peas or snow peas and the straw mushrooms and stir-fry 2 more minutes.

Mix the cornstarch with the soy sauce and stir this into ½ cup of water. Pour this liquid over the hot vegetables and let it bubble up and thicken while continuing to stir-fry a few seconds.

Immediately transfer to a warmed serving dish and garnish with scallions or herbs, if using.

STIR-FRIED BEANS WITH GARLIC

SERVES 4 AS AN ACCOMPANIMENT

2 tbsp vegetable oil
½ tsp salt
4 garlic cloves, coarsely chopped
1-inch cube of peeled fresh gingerroot, minced
1 lb green beans, cut into 3-inch lengths
½ cup chicken stock

Heat a wok over medium heat until hot, add the oil with the salt, garlic, and ginger, and stir-fry 30 seconds. Add the green beans and stock and continue to cook until the beans are just tender and most of the liquid has evaporated, about 4 minutes longer. Serve at once.

Stir-frying is the ideal healthy way to cook most vegetables. Use whatever is fresh and in season and try to make the best combination of colors, textures, and flavors.

Dainty QUAIL EGGS *are available fresh in some Asian markets. If you can't get them, you can substitute 4 chicken eggs, quartered or sliced. Do not warm them in the sauce – just add when serving.*

MUSHROOM CURRY WITH QUAIL EGGS

SERVES 4 AS A FIRST COURSE

2 tbsp vegetable oil
1 onion, chopped
1 garlic clove, minced
1-inch cube of peeled fresh gingerroot, minced
1 stalk of lemongrass, minced
2 hot chili peppers or more to taste, minced
grated zest and juice of 1 washed lime
1 tbsp finely chopped fresh cilantro stems
1 tsp salt
½ lb small button mushrooms
15 oz canned straw mushrooms, drained
1¼ cups canned coconut cream
24 hard-cooked quail eggs, shelled
chopped fresh cilantro, for garnish (optional)
chopped chili peppers, for garnish (optional)

Heat the oil in a heavy saucepan over medium heat and cook the onion until it is softened.

Add the garlic, ginger, lemongrass, chili peppers, lime zest, cilantro stems, and salt. Cook 1–2 minutes, stirring constantly.

Add the buttom mushrooms and cook until they are just beginning to soften, 3–4 minutes.

Add the straw mushrooms and the coconut cream and simmer, stirring occasionally, about 30 minutes.

Add the quail eggs and lime juice and cook 1–2 minutes longer, or until the eggs are heated through.

Pour into a warmed serving dish and garnish with chopped cilantro and chili peppers, if using.

CURRIED SWEET POTATO

SERVES 4 AS AN ACCOMPANIMENT

1 tbsp vegetable oil
1 onion, chopped
1 garlic clove, minced
grated zest of ½ washed lemon
1-inch piece of peeled fresh gingerroot, minced or crushed through a garlic press
1 tbsp curry powder
1 tsp turmeric
1¼ cups canned coconut cream
1½ lb sweet potato, peeled and cut into 1-inch cubes
½ tsp salt
⅓ cup plain yogurt
½ cup roughly chopped dry roasted peanuts, for garnish
finely chopped fresh cilantro or flat-leaf parsley, for garnish

Heat the oil in a heavy saucepan over medium heat and cook the onion until translucent. Add the garlic, lemon zest, ginger, and spices and stir-fry 2–3 minutes. Stir in the coconut cream and continue to cook 15 minutes over low heat, stirring occasionally.

Meanwhile, sprinkle the sweet potato with the salt and steam it until just tender, about 15 minutes. Do not over-cook.

Stir the yogurt into the sauce. Heat through, but do not boil. Mix the sweet potato into the curry sauce.

Transfer to a warmed serving dish or platter and garnish with the chopped peanuts and herbs.

Top: Curried Sweet Potato; bottom: Mushroom Curry with Quail Eggs served on a bed of noodles

The classic Japanese batter used in **Tempura Vegetables** produces the lightest possible coating. Use whatever selection of vegetables you fancy, or try slivers of meat or fish or raw shrimp, as the Japanese do.

FRIED NOODLES WITH VEGETABLES

SERVES 4 AS AN ACCOMPANIMENT

8 dried Chinese mushrooms
¾ lb Asian noodles
3 tbsp vegetable oil
1 garlic clove, thinly sliced
1-inch cube of peeled fresh gingerroot, minced
1 onion, chopped
1 small carrot, cut across at an angle into slices
½ green sweet pepper, seeded and cut into bite-sized
pieces
¾ cup sliced green cabbage
1 tbsp soy sauce
1 tbsp sesame oil
2 tbsp chopped raw shelled peanuts

Cover the dried mushrooms with hot water and let them soak 30 minutes. Drain and remove the hard stem (this can either be discarded or used to add flavor to stock). Slice the mushroom caps and reserve.

Cook the noodles according to the directions on the package and then drain well.

Heat the oil in a wok or large frying pan over medium heat and stir-fry the garlic and ginger 1 minute. Add the onion and stir-fry 2–3 minutes more. Then add the carrot, sweet pepper, cabbage, and sliced mushrooms caps and stir-fry 2–3 minutes.

Add the cooked and drained noodles and continue to cook 2–3 minutes, tossing all the ingredients together, until the noodles are thoroughly heated.

Stir in the soy sauce and sesame oil and sprinkle with the chopped nuts before serving.

Tempura Vegetables

TEMPURA VEGETABLES

SERVES 4 AS AN ACCOMPANIMENT

1 egg plus 1 egg yolk, beaten
¾ cup flour
about ½ lb mixed vegetables, such as zucchini,
asparagus tips, broccoli and cauliflower florets, baby
spinach leaves, carrots, and seeded sweet peppers, cut
into bite-sized pieces
vegetable oil, for deep-frying

In a bowl, make a smooth batter with the egg, egg yolk, flour, and about ¾ cup of water.

Dip the pieces of vegetable into the batter, then deep-fry in hot oil in a wok, a few at a time. Drain on paper towels and serve immediately as they are cooked, as they are or with a dipping sauce.

NOTE: Make a dipping sauce for this dish from equal quantities of soy sauce, fish sauce, and dry sherry, with a little grated fresh gingerroot.

Gado Gado, *a salad of cooked and raw vegetables with a spicy peanut dressing, is perhaps the best-known of all Indonesian dishes.* Nasi Goreng, *another typically Indonesian dish, consists of fried rice with chicken and shrimp – often topped with a fried egg or omelet – and is virtually a meal in itself. However, served together the two dishes make a wonderful well-balanced meal.*

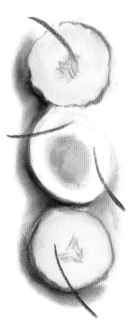

NASI GORENG

SERVES 4 AS A MAIN COURSE

2 cups long-grain rice
2 tbsp vegetable oil
¼ lb skinless boneless chicken breast, cut into small cubes
1 onion, chopped
2 garlic cloves, minced
1-inch cube of peeled fresh gingerroot, minced
1 hot chili pepper, seeded and finely chopped
½ tsp ground coriander seed
2 tbsp soy sauce
1 tbsp sugar
¼ lb peeled cooked small shrimp
1 egg, beaten, for garnish (optional)
cucumber slices, for garnish

About an hour or two ahead, cook the rice in boiling salted water until tender. Drain, if necessary, and then let it cool. This dish can be made successfully with leftover cooked rice, but it is much better if the rice is freshly cooked.

Heat the oil in a wok or large frying pan over medium heat and stir-fry the chicken and onion, together with the garlic, ginger, chili, and coriander, until the chicken is cooked and the onion slightly softened, 3–4 minutes.

Add the soy sauce, sugar, and shrimp and stir-fry 1 minute. Tip in the rice and stir-fry 2–3 minutes more.

If using the egg garnish, heat a very little oil in a small frying pan over medium heat and cook the beaten egg until just set. Then cut this omelet into strips.

Serve immediately, topped with the omelet strips, if using, and garnished with cucumber slices.

GADO GADO

SERVES 4 AS AN ACCOMPANIMENT

¾ lb green cabbage, shredded
5 oz green beans
¾ lb fresh bean sprouts
4 small new potatoes, cooked and sliced or quartered
¼ English cucumber, sliced
2 hard-cooked eggs, shelled and sliced or cut in small wedges
shrimp crackers, for garnish (optional)
FOR THE SAUCE
1 tbsp vegetable oil
1 small onion, chopped
1 garlic clove, minced
1 tsp chili powder
grated zest and 2 tsp juice from ½ small washed lemon
2 tsp brown sugar
1 tsp soy sauce
½ tsp salt
½ cup canned coconut cream
3 tbsp smooth peanut butter

First make the sauce: Heat the oil in a saucepan over medium heat and cook the onion with the garlic until translucent. Add the rest of the sauce ingredients with 6 tablespoons of water and simmer gently 15 minutes, stirring frequently and making sure the peanut butter dissolves. Let cool.

In a large pan of boiling salted water, blanch the cabbage and beans about 3 minutes and then blanch the bean sprouts 30 seconds only. Drain and refresh each batch under cold running water as soon as it is cooked. Drain again thoroughly and pat dry.

When the sauce is cool, arrange all the salad ingredients attractively in layers on a serving platter or on 4 plates, spoon over the sauce, and garnish with shrimp crackers, if using.

Top: Nasi Goreng; bottom: Gado Gado

Translucent CELLOPHANE NOODLES *are made from mung bean starch or rice flour rather than wheat and have a very delicate flavor. Bottled* CHINESE BLACK BEAN SAUCE, *made from fermented beans, is a widely used condiment in Chinese kitchens and is available from Asian markets and many supermarkets.*

CELLOPHANE NOODLES WITH BLACK BEAN SAUCE

SERVES 4 AS AN ACCOMPANIMENT

6 oz cellophane noodles
1 tbsp vegetable oil
1 large onion, thinly sliced
2 garlic cloves, minced
1 1/4 cups chicken stock
1 heaping tbsp Chinese black bean sauce
4 tsp light soy sauce
1/2 tsp chili powder
3/4 tsp Asian sesame oil

Soak the noodles in hot water for 10 minutes and then drain them well.

Heat the oil in a wok or large frying pan and stir-fry the onion 2 minutes. Add the garlic, stock, sauces, and chili powder and simmer 5 minutes.

Add the noodles and cook 2 minutes, stirring constantly. (They absorb most of the liquid.) Sprinkle over the sesame oil, toss, and serve at once.

SPICY COCONUT RICE

SERVES 4–6

2 2/3 cups basmati rice
1 tbsp vegetable oil
1 large onion, chopped
2 garlic cloves, chopped
1 tsp ground coriander seed
1 tsp ground cumin
1/4 tsp chili powder
1 1/2 tsp salt
2 1/2 cups thin canned coconut milk
chopped fresh cilantro or other herbs, for garnish

Rinse the rice thoroughly and drain well.

In a large heavy saucepan that has a tight-fitting lid, heat the oil over medium heat and fry the onion until softened. Add the garlic, spices, and salt and stir well. Add the rice and mix well until every grain is coated.

Add the coconut milk and bring to a boil. Turn the heat down to the lowest possible setting, put the lid tightly on the pan, and cook undisturbed about 15 minutes.

Without removing the lid, take the pan from the heat and set aside for 30 minutes to let the rice finish cooking in the steam.

Transfer to a serving dish and serve garnished with herbs.

Top: Spicy Coconut Rice; bottom: Cellophane Noodles with Black Bean Sauce

Of the many varieties of rice now widely available, basmati probably has the best flavor.

DESSERTS

*I*n the cuisines of the countries of the Far East the boundary between sweet and savory ingredients is much less marked than here in the West. For this reason, desserts and other sweet concoctions do not hold the same importance. Simple fresh fruit, in one form or another, usually makes the perfect refreshing finale to any Asian meal. However, here follow a few of my favorite unusual and delicious traditional sweet dishes, usually incorporating fresh fruit, in order to satisfy the Western sweet tooth and round off any type of meal. If short of time, any good fruit-based ice-cream or sorbet will also work well. Serve it with canned or fresh exotic fruit, or sprinkled with green ginger wine or passion fruit pulp.

Left: Balinese-Style Rice Pudding (page 61); right: Banana Pancake "Noodles" (page 60)

KEBABS OF TROPICAL FRUIT

SERVES 4

½ pineapple
1 banana
1 small wedge of watermelon
1 mango
½ papaya
1 kiwi fruit
juice of 1 lemon or lime

Peel, core, and seed the fruit as appropriate. Then cut them all into large bite-sized pieces.

Toss the fruit pieces in the lemon or lime juice to prevent discoloration.

Just before serving, thread the pieces of fruit alternately on wooden or metal skewers, contrasting colors attractively where possible.

BANANA PANCAKE "NOODLES"

SERVES 4

⅔ cup flour
pinch of salt
1 banana, peeled and mashed
2 eggs, beaten
⅔ cup milk
vegetable oil, for frying
sugar, for serving
juice of 1 lime, for serving
banana slices, for decoration (optional)

Mix the flour, salt, banana, eggs, and milk into a batter. (This is most easily done in a blender or food processor.) Let rest 1 hour.

Heat just enough oil in a medium-sized frying pan to coat the bottom with a thin film, then pour in one-quarter of the batter and cook over medium-low heat until pale gold on both sides, turning once. Keep this pancake warm while making 3 others in the same way. They must be cooked over low heat to let the centers cook through.

Roll up each pancake and quickly cut across at ½-inch intervals. Unroll to make long "noodles."

Make mounds of the "noodles" on 4 warmed plates. Sprinkle with sugar and a squeeze of lime juice and decorate with banana slices, if using.

BALINESE-STYLE RICE PUDDING

SERVES 4

2½ cups milk
1¼ cups canned coconut cream
¼ cup short-grain rice
¼ cup packed brown sugar
6 cardamom pods, split
2 tbsp butter, cut in small pieces, plus more for greasing
¼ tsp grated nutmeg
curls of fresh coconut, peeled with a swivel-bladed vegetable peeler, for garnish
salad of tropical fruits, such as mangoes, guavas, pineapples, bananas, limes, and passion fruit, for serving

Preheat the oven to 300°F and grease a shallow baking dish with butter.

Put the milk, coconut cream, rice, sugar, cardamom pods, and butter in the prepared dish. Bake 3 hours, stirring the contents of the dish every hour.

Remove from the oven, stir in the nutmeg, and let cool. Chill until required.

Serve chilled, garnished with coconut curls and accompanied by a tropical fruit salad.

ORANGES IN GREEN GINGER WINE

SERVES 4

4 large oranges
about ⅔ cup green ginger wine
1 tbsp sliced almonds

Peel the oranges, removing all the bitter white pith, and slice across the sections as thinly as possible. Arrange the slices in an attractive serving dish.

Pour over enough ginger wine to almost cover the oranges. Cover the bowl and chill several hours, or overnight if possible.

Just before serving, sprinkle the sliced almonds on top.

GREEN GINGER WINE *is a British brew that is available in some liquor stores and specialty grocers. It gives a flavor quite like that of many Asian preparations.*

Fresh lychees make
GUAVA GELATIN
WITH LYCHEES
even more
memorable. In fact,
any form of fresh or
canned exotic fruit
can be substituted.

GUAVA GELATIN WITH LYCHEES

SERVES 4

14 oz canned guavas in syrup
2 tbsp unflavored gelatin
14 oz canned lychees in syrup

Drain the syrup from the guavas, measure it, and place in a bowl.

Following the directions on the package, dissolve half the gelatin in enough water to make the syrup measure 1¼ cups. Mix this with the syrup and pour the mixture into a small square pan or mold that has been rinsed in cold water. Chill until set.

Meanwhile, purée the guavas in a blender or food processor and then strain the purée.

Dissolve the rest of the gelatin in sufficient water to make the puréed guavas measure 1¼ cups. Mix this with the purée, then pour this mixture over the jellied syrup mixture in the pan to make a second layer. Return to the refrigerator and chill until completely set, preferably overnight.

Dip the pan briefly in hot water and unmold the gelatin. Using a hot wet knife, cut the gelatin into cubes. Serve the cubes mixed with the lychees and their syrup.

Top: Oranges in Green Ginger Wine (page 61); bottom: Guava Gelatin with Lychees

INDEX

Page numbers in *italic* refer to the photographs

ACKNOWLEDGMENTS

The author would particularly like to thank Michelle Garrett for taking such wonderful photographs, Mary Evans and Sue Storey for designing the book so beautifully, and Ian Hands for his invaluable help in preparing the food for photography.